Take-Along Guide

Frogs, Toads and Turtles

by Diane L. Burns
illustrations by Linda Garrow

NORTHWORD
Minnetonka, Minnesota

DEDICATION

To Clint and Andy, who have had these creatures in hand
at one time or another. Pass along the wonder.

ACKNOWLEDGMENTS

Special thanks to Jim and Kirsten Kranz and Dawn Bassuener,
whose knowledge, expertise in the field, and patience in answering my many
questions are greatly appreciated.

© Diane L. Burns, 1997

NorthWord Books for Young Readers
11571 K-Tel Drive
Minnetonka, MN 55343
1-888-255-9989
www.tnkidsbooks.com

Illustrations by Linda Garrow
Book design by Lisa Moore

Library of Congress Cataloging-in-Publication Data

Burns, Diane L.

    Frogs, toads, and turtles / by Diane L. Burns; illustrated by Linda Garrow.
          p.   cm.—(Take-along guide)
    ISBN 1-55971-593-6 (sc)
        1. Frogs—Juvenile literature.   2. Toads—Juvenile literature.
3. Turtles—Juvenile literature.   [1. Frogs.   2. Toads.   3. Turtles.]   I. Garrow, Linda,
ill.   II. Title.   III. Series.
QL668.E2B865   1997
597.8—dc21   96-37143

Printed in Malaysia

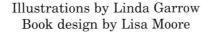

CONTENTS

INTRODUCTION

Frogs, toads and turtles are alike in some ways. All three are cold-blooded, which means their body temperature is the same as the air around them. To stay cool, they burrow underground or underwater. To warm up, they bask in the sun.

These animals all have four legs and a head, but no teeth. They don't have ears like people and some other animals have. Instead, they hear with an organ called a tympanum.

Frogs, toads and turtles are also different in some ways. Frogs and toads shed their skins as they grow, and most do not have a tail. A turtle does have a tail but does not shed its skin. And a turtle has a hard shell to protect it.

When turtle eggs hatch, little turtles come out. When frog and toad eggs hatch, tadpoles swim out. The tadpoles then turn into frogs or toads by metamorphosis.

Turtles stretch their long necks to help them see in all directions. Frogs and toads have bulgy eyes that can see all around them.

Frogs and toads "talk" by pulling air from the lungs into a vocal sac that makes the throat swell like a balloon. As the air travels past the vocal chords, it makes sound. A turtle can grunt or hiss, but it is much quieter than a frog or toad.

Have fun exploring the amazing world of Frogs, Toads and Turtles!

FROGS

Frogs are amphibians. They can live on land and in the water. Some are even found in trees. They are often together in groups.

Most frogs have sleek bodies with smooth skin. Rather than drinking through their mouths, frogs absorb water through their skin, which must be moist to keep them alive.

Frogs do not have ribs. They make soft landings on their chests when they leap. Frogs can jump longer than the length of their bodies. And for its size, a frog can swim 10 times faster than the fastest human swimmer.

There are several ways that frogs defend themselves from danger. They are slippery to catch and hold. They dive deep and stay underwater for long periods of time. They leap away from danger. Their skin color and markings help them to hide. Some may play dead. Others puff up to make themselves seem bigger.

BULLFROG

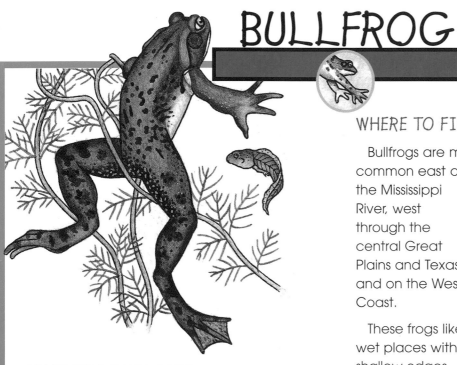

WHAT IT LOOKS LIKE

These frogs are wide and grow up to 7 inches long.

Their smooth, dull green to brown skin often has dark spots. The belly is whitish, sometimes with dark marks.

The back feet are webbed.

WHERE TO FIND IT

Bullfrogs are most common east of the Mississippi River, west through the central Great Plains and Texas and on the West Coast.

These frogs like wet places with shallow edges and overhanging brush, such as ponds, lakes and reservoirs.

On hot days, a bullfrog basks in shallow water with only its eyes showing. In winter, bullfrogs hibernate in the mud of riverbanks and lakes.

Their call is a deep, echoing croak: "*Chug-a-rumm*" and "*Knee-deep.*"

WHAT IT EATS

Bullfrogs feed at night. They eat mice, crayfish, salamanders, small birds, snakes, snails, crabs, fish, tadpoles and other frogs.

Don't hurry.
Take your time and have fun!

LEOPARD FROG

WHAT IT LOOKS LIKE

Leopard frogs are slender. They grow to be 2 to 4 inches long.

Their smooth skin is green or brown with dark, round spots. A green-yellow line runs from each eye down its back. Two ridges run down the middle of its back. The belly is yellow-white and may be spotted.

The leopard frog's back toes are webbed.

WHERE TO FIND IT

Leopard frogs are found throughout the United States except on the West Coast.

Leopard frogs live in groups along the wet edges of ponds, lakes and streams. They are also found in wet meadows when the grass is high.

During hot weather, they bask on lily pads. In winter, leopard frogs hibernate by burrowing into the bottoms of lakes and ponds.

Their short call sounds like fingers rubbing across a balloon.

WHAT IT EATS

This frog eats during dusk and nighttime. It likes spiders, wood lice, worms, flies and moths.

INTERESTING FACTS

This frog's name comes from the pattern of its skin.

Look for frogs in quiet, undisturbed water.

SPRING PEEPER

WHAT IT LOOKS LIKE

This small frog grows up to 1 1/2 inches long.

Its smooth skin is olive-green, tan or gray. Across its back is a marking that looks like an "X." The belly is reddish to yellowish.

Each toe has a tiny suction pad.

WHERE TO FIND IT

This treefrog is found everywhere east of the Mississippi River south to northern Florida, and west into Texas.

Spring peepers like the low edges of still, shallow water. They like woodland ponds, too. They cling to branches or blades of grass above the waterline.

Spring peepers hibernate under leaves and behind tree bark.

Their high trilling chorus sounds like jingle bells.

INTERESTING FACTS

The sound made by this tiny treefrog can carry as far as a half-mile!

WHAT IT EATS

Spring peepers eat at night. They like aphids, mosquitoes and small worms.

Use patience and sharp eyesight to find frogs.

CHORUS FROG

WHERE TO FIND IT

Chorus frogs are found from the Rocky Mountains, across the Great Plains to the East Coast, south to Georgia and west to Arizona.

This frog likes grassy edges of riverbanks, ponds and shallow swamps.

In cold places, they hibernate by burrowing under leaves.

Their raspy trill is especially noisy after a rainstorm.

WHAT IT LOOKS LIKE

Chorus frogs are slender with pointed snouts. They grow no more than 2 inches long.

Their smooth skin can be greenish-gray to brown. There is a dark stripe that starts at the mouth and goes through each eye. The belly is whitish and looks bumpy.

Some chorus frogs have dark, broken stripes down the back. Others have dark blotches or bright green spots rimmed with black.

Each toe has a small suction pad.

WHAT IT EATS

Chorus frogs eat mosquitoes and flies at dusk and nighttime.

10

Tell an adult where you are going, or take one with you.

CRICKET FROG

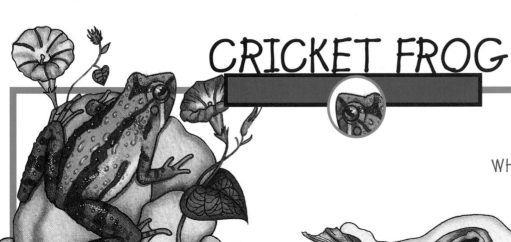

WHAT IT LOOKS LIKE

Cricket frogs are from 1/2 to 1 1/4 inches long.

They have rough, green or brown skin. Sometimes, there are darker reddish-brown markings on the back and legs. The belly is creamy. Some have a white stripe below the eye.

There is usually a red or green streak down the center of the back and a dark triangle shape on top of the head.

The cricket frog's back feet are webbed.

WHERE TO FIND IT

Cricket frogs are mostly found east of the Mississippi River.

Cricket frogs love shady places under leaves and overhanging branches around quiet pools and ponds.

In the cold north, they hibernate under leaves and logs.

The chorus frog's call sounds like two marbles tapped together. It goes faster and faster: "*Kick-kick-kick.*"

WHAT IT EATS

Cricket frogs eat spiders, flies and aphids during the day.

INTERESTING FACTS

This frog's name comes from its insect-like chirp.

It lives on the ground and does not climb.

Don't approach or touch any wild animals you might see.

GREEN FROG

WHERE TO FIND IT

Green frogs are found east of the Mississippi River as far south as Florida and west to Texas.

They live along the edges of streams, springs, ponds and swamps.

Green frogs hibernate in winter, burrowing into stream banks and the bottoms of ponds.

Its call sounds like the twanging of a banjo string.

WHAT IT LOOKS LIKE

This chunky frog grows to be 2 to 4 inches long.

Its green or brown skin may be rough or smooth.

It has dark brown spots and blotches on the back and legs, and a ridge along each side of the back. The belly is white with dark spots. Male green frogs have a yellowish throat.

The back toes are webbed.

WHAT IT EATS

Green frogs eat at night. They like water insects, and also those flying just above the water's surface, such as dragonflies.

INTERESTING FACTS

This frog some-times rests in shallow water, floating on its stomach with legs dangling down.

Don't chase frogs away from their homes.

WOOD FROG

WHAT IT LOOKS LIKE

Wood frogs grow from 1 1/2 to 3 inches long.

Their pinkish or brownish bodies are chunky. Their legs are long. The belly is lighter than the body.

A dark stripe with white edges runs from the eye along each side of the back. The eyes look like they have a dark mask across them.

The wood frog's back toes are webbed.

WHERE TO FIND IT

Wood frogs live in the North into Alaska. They are also found in the eastern United States, west as far as Wisconsin and into the southeastern mountains.

They like wet woods and grasslands, near water, but usually not in it.

During hot weather, wood frogs hide beneath fallen leaves and logs. They hibernate in winter beneath stones and logs.

They call from woodland ponds, just before late-winter ice melts. Their call sounds like "*Kraack-arrack.*"

WHAT IT EATS

Wood frogs eat worms, insects and snails during the day.

INTERESTING FACTS

This frog lives as far north as the Arctic Circle!

In one leap, it can jump five feet.

Sit quietly away from the water's edge to see frogs.

PACIFIC TREEFROG

WHAT IT LOOKS LIKE

Pacific treefrogs grow to be 1 to 2 inches long. They have slender heads.

Their rough-skinned body is mossy gray, green or brown, often with darker spots. The belly is whitish.

A dark stripe runs from the nose and through each eye to the front legs.

This treefrog has sticky toe pads. Its back feet are slightly webbed.

WHERE TO FIND IT

Pacific treefrogs live along the West Coast from Washington to California, eastward into Montana, Idaho, Nevada, Utah and Arizona.

They are found on the ground or among plants at the edges of streams, ditches and ponds. They also live in burrows and rock crevices.

When very warm, they hide between the bark and wood of fallen tree trunks. They hibernate under stones and in logs and bark.

Its call is a musical, 2-note chorus, with the second note higher than the first: "*Kreck-ek, kreck-ek.*"

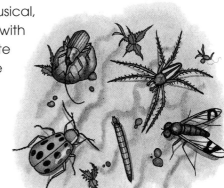

WHAT IT EATS

Pacific treefrogs eat flies, small worms, beetles and spiders at dusk and nighttime.

INTERESTING FACTS

This treefrog can change its body color to match what it is sitting on or near.

Be aware of everything around you.

GRAY TREEFROG

WHAT IT LOOKS LIKE

Gray treefrogs are chunky. They have wide heads and grow to be 1 1/2 to 2 inches long.

Their rough, bumpy skin is gray or green with dark blotches on the back. They have a yellowish spot under each eye.

The belly is whitish or gray. The inside of the back legs is orange.

The toes have suction pads. The back feet are webbed.

WHAT IT EATS

At night, this frog eats the insects it finds in cracks and crevices of tree bark.

WHERE TO FIND IT

Gray treefrogs live in every state east of the Mississippi River. They live as far west as Minnesota, south through Kansas and into Texas.

They like open, shallow water with trees standing in it.

In cold places, they hibernate under tree bark.

Its musical trill sounds like a calling bird: "*Wit-wit-wit.*"

INTERESTING FACTS

Gray treefrogs live in trees almost their whole lives.

Their skin looks like tree bark with moss.

15

GREEN TREEFROG

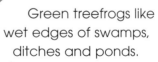

This treefrog is nicknamed the "rain frog" because it often sings before a thunderstorm.

Green treefrogs like wet edges of swamps, ditches and ponds. Sometimes they can be found on lighted windows at night.

These frogs don't hibernate. They can be found all year long.

Its call often sounds like the "*Quonk*" of a cowbell.

WHAT IT LOOKS LIKE

Green treefrogs have smooth skin and pointed heads. They grow to be 1 1/2 to 2 1/4 inches long. Their slender bodies and legs may be bright green, gray-green or yellow.

A creamy stripe runs from the mouth along each side of its body. Sometimes, there are also tiny yellow-orange spots on the back.

The belly is yellow-white and bumpy.

Its toes have suction cups. The back feet are webbed.

WHAT IT EATS

Green treefrogs eat flies, mosquitoes and other insects.

WHERE TO FIND IT

It lives along the Atlantic Coast from New Jersey to Texas. It is also found in the South and along the Mississippi River as far north as Illinois.

Get permission before going onto someone's land.

MAKE A FROG PUZZLE

You can have a frog with you anytime you want, by making your own frog puzzle. Here's how:

WHAT YOU NEED

- A plain white piece of flat, stiff cardboard

- Fine-lined markers in a variety of colors or a box of crayons

- Scissors

- An empty shoe box

WHAT TO DO

1 Using the markers or crayons, draw your favorite frog on the cardboard. Make the drawing as large as you can without going off the edges. You can draw the frog hopping, sitting, eating, sleeping or swimming.

2 Color in the animal, including its spots, blotches and lines.

3 Using a marker or a crayon, draw squiggly lines all across the picture. Let the lines go in different directions and from edge to edge. (HINT: For an easy puzzle with big pieces, draw only a few lines far apart. For a harder puzzle, draw lots of lines close together).

4 Cut the picture apart into its puzzle pieces using the scissors.

Mix up all the pieces. Now you are ready to have fun putting your frog back together!

When you are finished playing with your puzzle, you can store the pieces in the shoe box.

TOADS

Toads are amphibians like frogs. But toads prefer dry land. They would rather be near water than in it. They are often found by themselves rather than in a group.

Their bodies are chubby and their skin is rough and bumpy. It is dry, not moist or slippery.

Toads have short, thick legs. They only hop distances shorter than the length of their bodies.

A toad's color helps it hide from enemies. Another toad defense is that their skin tastes bad to enemies that might try to eat them.

Some people think that you can get warts from toads, but that's not true. Toads don't even have warts, they just have bumps on their skin.

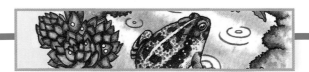

AMERICAN TOAD

WHAT IT LOOKS LIKE

The American toad grows to be 2 to 4 inches long. It has a pudgy body. It has a large, blunt head and nose. Some have yellow throats.

The skin looks paint-splattered. It is brownish-green to red-brown, and may have a light stripe on the back. It often has large spots with bumps on the back. The light belly has smaller bumps.

There are often dark spots on its legs and sides.

WHERE TO FIND IT

American toads live in the eastern United States from New England south to Georgia, west to Oklahoma and north into Minnesota.

They like gardens and fields, and stay cool beneath woodpiles and stones.

They are more active at night than during the day. They hibernate in their burrows.

Its call is a deep whistle lasting up to a half-minute: "*Burrrr . . .*"

WHAT IT EATS

This toad eats crickets, flies, locusts, sow bugs, worms and beetles.

INTERESTING FACTS

This toad digs backward into its burrow at hibernating time.

Watch where you step.

EASTERN SPADEFOOT TOAD

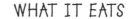

WHAT IT LOOKS LIKE

This short, fat toad grows to be 2 to 2 1/2 inches long.

The smoothish, brown skin has a few bumps. It usually has 2 yellowish stripes down its back. The belly is grayish-white.

The short, thick legs have broad, webbed back feet. Each back foot has a "spade" on it that helps them dig their burrows.

WHAT IT EATS

This toad eats flies, spiders and ants.

INTERESTING FACTS

This toad can absorb so much water through its skin that it swells like a little balloon.

WHERE TO FIND IT

Eastern spadefoot toads are found in sandy places along the Atlantic Coast from Massachusetts to Florida, and west to Texas. They also live down the Ohio River to Missouri and Arkansas.

They are active at night, especially after a heavy rain. They stay in their burrows during the day. They hibernate in cold northern areas.

Their short call is a harsh, crow-like "*Whaarh*!"

SPECIAL WARNING

Do not touch spadefoot toads. They can make your skin burn.

GREAT PLAINS TOAD

WHERE TO FIND IT

This toad lives across the Great Plains from western Minnesota to the Rocky Mountains, south to Texas and across the Southwest into California.

It likes the edges of ditches and grassy river bottoms.

It is active usually at night, and burrows into the ground during the day. It hibernates in cold areas.

The piercing, low call sounds like a toy horn. It can last 20 seconds or more.

WHAT IT LOOKS LIKE

Great Plains toads are chubby and grow to be 2 to 4 inches long.

The gray-brown to green-yellow skin looks bumpy. Most have pairs of large, dark blotches with light edges. They usually have a creamy stripe on the back.

Young toads have a "V" marking between the eyes.

Their feet are light with dark tips.

WHAT IT EATS

Great Plains toads eat slugs, spiders, moths, flies, beetles and grubs.

INTERESTING FACTS

To call, this toad inflates a sac on its neck bigger than its head.

Take drinking water with you when you go exploring.

21

WOODHOUSE'S TOAD

They like swampy edges, slow rivers, ditches, reservoirs, cattle tanks and backyards.

They are more active at night than during the day. They hibernate by burrowing in loose soil and under plants and leaves.

Its sweet, short call sounds like the chuckling bleat of a sheep: "*Blaahh.....*"

WHAT IT LOOKS LIKE

This toad grows to be 2 to 4 inches long.

Its skin is olive-brown to greenish-gray. A whitish stripe runs down the center of the back. At least 1 large bump is in each dark spot on its back. The sides have dark spots, too.

Its head is thick and wide with a blunt nose. Its belly is tannish-yellow, usually without spots.

The tips of the toes are dark.

WHAT IT EATS

Woodhouse's toads are attracted to lights at night, where they find moths, worms, slugs and mosquitoes.

WHERE TO FIND IT

Woodhouse's toads live across the Great Plains south to Texas, Nevada and California. They are also found across the Southwest.

Wear boots, gloves and long pants.

OAK TOAD

WHERE TO FIND IT

This toad likes scrubby pine areas from North Carolina to Florida, and west to Louisiana.

It is found under boards or logs, in small burrows, or near shallow pools that fill with water after a thunderstorm.

Oak toads are active during the day, especially after a heavy, warm rain.

These toads don't hibernate, so you may see them all year.

Oak toads have a chicken-like call that lasts about 10 seconds.

WHAT IT EATS

Oak toads like insects such as spiders, flies and ants.

WHAT IT LOOKS LIKE

Oak toads are chunky. They grow from 3/4 to 1 1/4 inches long.

The bumpy skin is gray to blackish with golden spots. There is a yellow-white stripe down the back.

Pairs of tan to black spots run from the eyes down the back. The belly is creamy-gray.

The legs have black bands.

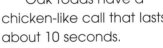

Interesting Facts

This is the smallest toad in North America.

23

Use the ruler on the back of this book to measure what you find.

FOWLER'S TOAD

WHAT IT LOOKS LIKE

The chubby Fowler's toad grows to be 2 to 3 inches long. It has a short, wide head.

The skin is gray-brown, greenish or brick red. There are dark spots with black edges. At least 3 bumps are in each large dark spot. There is also a light yellow stripe down the back.

The tan belly and chest usually have no spots.

It has long legs and long, slender toes.

WHERE TO FIND IT

Fowler's toads live along the Atlantic Coast from New Hampshire to North Carolina and west to Michigan. They are also found on the Gulf Coast from Louisiana to Oklahoma and north to Illinois.

They like warm, sandy edges around lakeshores, river valleys and ditches. They also like pastures, fields, gardens and sand dunes.

They come out after a warm, heavy rain and are active day and night. They hibernate in cold areas.

Its call is a dull buzz that can last up to 4 seconds. It sounds like "Waaahh."

WHAT IT EATS

Fowler's toads eat slugs, beetles, worms, flies, aphids and spiders.

INTERESTING FACTS

Toads don't drink water very often. Most of it comes from the food they eat.

Wear a hat and use sunscreen to protect yourself from the sun.

SOUTHERN TOAD

WHERE TO FIND IT

Southern toads live from North Carolina to Florida, and west to Texas.

They like sandy fields and scrubby pine places. They are usually found near water, but not in it.

These toads do not hibernate. They are active more at dusk and at night than during the day.

The call is a high-pitched trill that lasts about 7 seconds.

WHAT IT LOOKS LIKE

This chunky toad grows to be 1 1/2 to 3 1/2 inches long.

The body is creamy-gray to reddish-black. The skin is rough and bumpy.

There are often dark streaks, blotches and stripes on its body. There is also a light stripe down the back. The belly is grayish.

It has slender feet and toes.

WHAT IT EATS

Southern toads like fireflies, locusts, spiders, crickets, grubs and small worms.

Watch for changes in weather.

25

MAKE A TOAD HOUSE

Toads like cool, moist places. You can make them a "house"
that they will want to use during hot, dry weather.

WHAT YOU NEED

- A sheet of newspaper
- A chipped or cracked plastic flowerpot
- A pair of heavy scissors
- A permanent marker
- A fist-sized rock

WHAT TO DO

1 Spread the newspaper over your work area.

2 Using the marker, draw a doorway at the open edge of the flowerpot about the size of a silver dollar.

3 Using the scissors, cut carefully along the marked line. You may need an adult's help.

4 Take both the flowerpot and the rock outside. Put the flowerpot upside-down in a cool, shady area where it won't be bothered.

5 Pile loose dirt around the pot, but not across the doorway.

6 Put the rock on the flowerpot to help to hold it down all year long.

26

Your toad house is now ready for its special guest!

TURTLES

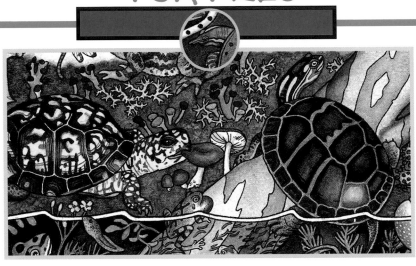

Turtles are reptiles. They move slowly on land compared to other animals. But they are swift and graceful in water.

Most turtles like freshwater lakes, ponds and rivers. They are also found on the land surrounding these and other wet places. Some turtles live in the ocean. Still others, called tortoises, prefer to stay on dry land all the time.

A turtle's favorite thing to do during the daytime is "bask." That means they like to rest and soak up warmth on top of a log or rock, or even each other!

The turtle's shell makes up as much as a third of the turtle's total weight. The shell is connected at the sides, with openings for the head, tail and legs.

Turtle shells are either bony or leathery. Some are rounded like an upside-down bowl. Others are almost flat. Whatever its shape, the shell protects the turtle's soft body.

To protect themselves from danger, some turtles can pull in their head and legs and hide inside their shells. Others can bite, hiss or scratch. So always be careful and don't get too close.

SNAPPING TURTLE

INTERESTING FACTS

Snapping turtles often let other turtles bask on their backs.

WHERE TO FIND IT

Snappers live across the eastern, central and Gulf coastal United States, through Texas and west to Colorado, Wyoming and Montana.

They like shallow freshwater lakes, rivers and ponds. They also can be found along the soft bottoms and edges of deep water, such as reservoirs.

Snapping turtles are active day and night, floating on the water or creeping along the bottom. They hibernate in muddy lake and river bottoms.

WHAT IT LOOKS LIKE

This turtle can weigh 75 pounds and grow to be 2 feet long.

Its tan, olive-green or black shell has scallops along the rear edge. Young turtles have several rows of low, ridged bumps. Older turtles may have bumps that have been worn smooth. The turtle's underside is yellow-tan.

Its skin is tan to gray-black. The broad head is often covered with algae.

The thick legs have webbed toes, and claws. The long tail has thick saw-teeth on the edges.

WHAT IT EATS

Snapping turtles eat insects, crabs, fish, frogs, birds, snakes and plants.

SPECIAL WARNING

DO NOT TOUCH.
This turtle bites hard and fast!

29

ALLIGATOR SNAPPING TURTLE

WHAT IT LOOKS LIKE

This turtle can grow to be 200 pounds and over 2 feet long, though most are much smaller.

The shell has rows of peaked ridges down its back. The shell is golden-brown to gray-green. The underside is yellow.

The skin is gray-black to tan. The head is large with a hooked beak.

The thick legs have webbed toes with claws. The long tail is thick.

WHERE TO FIND IT

Alligator snapping turtles live along the Gulf Coast from Georgia to Texas, and the Mississippi River valley north to Indiana and Illinois, west to Kansas.

They like the deep, quiet water of muddy rivers, lakes, canals and sloughs where they often lie on the bottom.

They are active day and night. They hibernate in cold climates inside muskrat lodges or under banks.

WHAT IT EATS

Alligator snappers eat fish, small alligators and water birds, clams, snakes, frogs and some plants.

INTERESTING FACTS

The alligator snapper "fishes" by opening its mouth underwater and wiggling a pink, worm-like piece of its tongue!

SPECIAL WARNING

DO NOT TOUCH. Snappers bite hard!

WESTERN PAINTED TURTLE

WHERE TO FIND IT

Western painted turtles live from Wisconsin and Illinois west across the Great Plains to Washington and Oregon.

They like slow-moving rivers and streams, with rocks or logs for basking.

They are active during early morning and late afternoon. They bask in groups at midday and sleep underwater at night.
They hibernate under banks or in the muddy bottoms of pools and rivers.

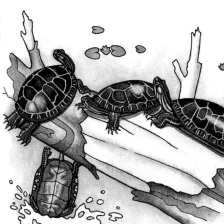

WHAT IT LOOKS LIKE

Western painted turtles grow to be 4 to 9 inches long.

The shell is olive-green to black, with short, light bars around the edge. Yellow lines divide the smooth shell so that it looks like puzzle pieces.

The underside is reddish, with a dark blotch that spreads out at the edges.

The green skin has yellow and red streaks on the head and legs. The small head usually has a yellow spot behind each eye.

The clawed feet are webbed. The tail is short.

WHAT IT EATS

Western painted turtles eat water plants, leeches, crabs and clams.

Treat all animals with respect.

WOOD TURTLE

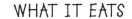

WHAT IT LOOKS LIKE

Wood turtles grow to be 8 inches long.

The rough shell looks like it is made up of little pyramids with black or yellow rings. The underside is yellow with brown blotches.

A wood turtle's skin is orange-red on top and tan-brown beneath. The black head is sleek and long.

The clawed feet are not webbed. The tail is medium-long.

WHAT IT EATS

Wood turtles eat worms, tadpoles, insects, berries and fungi.

WHERE TO FIND IT

Wood turtles live from New England to Virginia and across the upper Great Lakes west to Minnesota and Iowa.

They like moist woods and are often near water, not in it.

Wood turtles bask at midday on logs and sunny stream banks. They are active during early morning and late afternoon.

They hibernate in bottom mud or under logs in woods.

INTERESTING FACTS

Wood turtles are protected in some states.

Sometimes this turtle stamps its front feet on the ground and eats the earthworms that pop up.

Don't put your hand into any hole or burrow. It may be an animal's home.

SPINY SOFTSHELL TURTLE

WHAT IT LOOKS LIKE

Spiny softshell turtles grow to be 20 inches long and can weigh up to 35 pounds.

The flat, olive-brown shell is hard, with softer edges. The shell looks like a pancake and feels like sandpaper. There are small, dark, spots on it and short spines on the front edge. The underside is usually light with a dark blotch.

The turtle's skin is olive to orange on top and gray-white underneath. It has a long neck. Its slender head has a tubelike snout. A yellow stripe runs up each side of the neck and through the eye.

The tail is short. The webbed feet have claws.

WHERE TO FIND IT

Spiny softshells live in the eastern, central and south-eastern United States, across the central Plains, west to Wyoming, Nevada and Texas. They are rare in the Northeast.

Softshells are active day and night, along shallow rivers and streams with swift currents.

They bask on sand banks and floating plants. In cold climates, they hibernate in bottom mud.

WHAT IT EATS

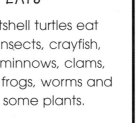

Softshell turtles eat insects, crayfish, minnows, clams, frogs, worms and some plants.

INTERESTING FACTS

Softshell turtles rest underwater, breathing through snouts that reach to the surface. They also breathe through their skin.

Be kind to all animals.

BOX TURTLE

WHAT IT LOOKS LIKE

Box turtles grow to be 4 to 7 inches long.

The olive-brown to dark brown shell is longer than it is wide. Eastern box turtle shells have orange or olive-green blotches. Others have yellow lines.

The underside is yellow with dark green streaks or smudges. The turtle's skin is gray-green to red-black with yellow or red-orange streaks. The head is chunky.

The tail is very short. The clawed feet are not webbed.

WHERE TO FIND IT

Eastern box turtles like open, moist woods south of the Great Lakes and the Mississippi River eastward to the Atlantic Coast. Other types of box turtles live in the plains and grasslands of the southwestern, central and south-central United States.

Box turtles live on land. They hide beneath damp, rotten logs during dry weather. They come out after a rain, sometimes to soak in mud. They are active during the day.

In cold areas, they hibernate in burrows, stumps or mud.

WHAT IT EATS

Box turtles eat worms, slugs, insects and snails. Some also eat the fruits, flowers, roots, seeds and leaves of plants.

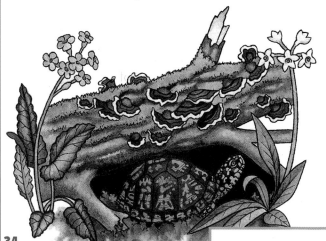

Don't leave behind any litter.

MAP TURTLE

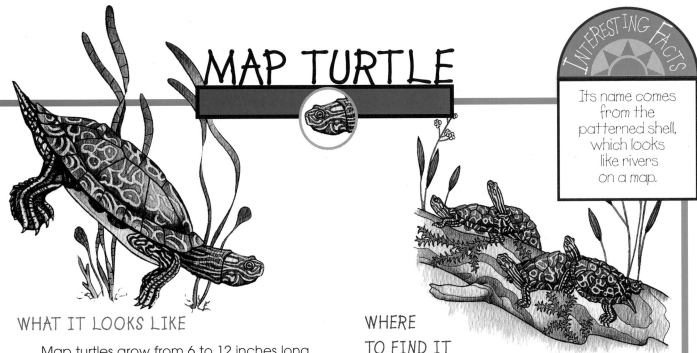

INTERESTING FACTS

Its name comes from the patterned shell, which looks like rivers on a map.

WHAT IT LOOKS LIKE

Map turtles grow from 6 to 12 inches long.

The mossy-green or brownish shell is flat and smooth with a ridge down the middle. It has thin yellow lines. The shell is jagged along the rear edge.

The skin is dark green with bright yellow stripes. Adult map turtles have a creamy yellow underside. Young turtles have a dark pattern underneath.

They have slender heads with a yellow spot behind each eye.

The tail is short. The feet are webbed and have claws.

WHERE TO FIND IT

Map turtles live in the Great Lakes region and along the Mississippi River. They are also found from the Ohio River valley to New England, south to Tennessee and Arkansas.

They like slow-moving rivers and lakes with floating logs and large rocks for sunning.

They are active in the morning and late afternoon. At midday, they gather to bask, often on top of one another. They hibernate in bottom mud.

WHAT IT EATS

Some types of map turtles eat only shellfish such as clams, crayfish and snails. Others eat insects, worms and some plants.

Watch out for poison ivy and poison oak.

35

BLANDING'S TURTLE

INTERESTING FACTS

Blanding's turtles are protected in some states.

This shy turtle spends all of its time in the water except when it basks.

WHERE TO FIND IT

Blanding's turtles live in northern New England and west across the northern Great Lakes as far as Nebraska and South Dakota.

They like quiet streams and ponds, and marshes and sloughs with clean, firm bottoms. They bask on logs, muskrat houses, steep banks and driftwood.

Blanding's turtles are active during the day, especially in the morning. They sleep on pond bottoms or in floating plants at night. They hibernate in muskrat lodges and bottom mud.

WHAT IT LOOKS LIKE

Blanding's turtles grow to be 6 to 9 inches long.

The shiny, domed shell is dark black-green with many yellow speckles that can run together like streaks. The underside is yellow with green blotches along the edges.

The skin is green-gray. The head is sleek and small with a long neck. The jaw and neck are yellow underneath.

The webbed feet have claws. The tail is medium-long.

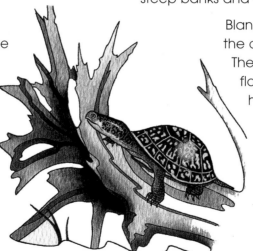

WHAT IT EATS

This turtle eats crayfish, frogs, insects, snails, worms and plants.

Be careful of turtles crossing the road.

RED-EARED TURTLE

WHAT IT LOOKS LIKE

Red-ears grow up to 9 inches long.

Its olive-brown shell is smooth and oval. It is splotched with red and yellow lines on its back. The rear edge of the shell is jagged. The yellowish underside has solid dark spots down its center.

The skin is olive-brown with orange-yellow stripes. Its small head has a red or yellow patch and stripe behind each eye.

The thick tail is medium-long. The webbed feet have claws.

WHERE TO FIND IT

Red-ears live from the mid-Atlantic states to the Gulf Coast and west into New Mexico. They are also found in the Mississippi River valley.

Red-ears like quiet, slow-moving rivers and ponds with muddy bottoms.

They are active in the morning and late afternoon. Red-ears rest at midday and at night. They bask on logs on top of one another.

Red-eared turtles hibernate in very cold weather, using muskrat lodges or underwater burrows. They come out to bask on warmer winter days.

WHAT IT EATS

Young red-ears eat insects, frogs, crayfish, and worms. Adults prefer plants such as duckweed and algae.

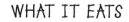

Use insect repellent to protect yourself.

EASTERN MUD TURTLE

WHERE TO FIND IT

Eastern mud turtles are found along the Atlantic Coast from New England to the Gulf Coast, and west to Louisiana. They also live in the Midwest from Illinois east to Pennsylvania. They are most common in parts of the southeastern states.

They like shallow, soft-bottomed bays, sloughs, canals, marshes and ponds, with lots of plants.

These turtles are active in the morning and evening. They do not bask much. Instead they crawl along the watery bottom or walk on land.

In northern areas, they hibernate in bottom mud, in burrows, or under plants.

WHAT IT LOOKS LIKE

Mud turtles grow up to 4 inches long.

The smooth, oval shell is yellow-brown to black. It looks like it's divided into pieces of a jigsaw puzzle. The underside is orange to yellow-brown and usually has a black center with dark blotches.

The skin is olive-brown and blotchy. It has a chunky head.

All four feet are webbed and have claws. The mud turtle has a short, thick tail.

INTERESTING Facts

Mud turtles smell like wet earth.

WHAT IT EATS

Mud turtles eat water insect larvae, crabs, clams and fish. Some also eat algae and water plants.

Use the Scrapbook to draw what you see.

GOPHER TORTOISE

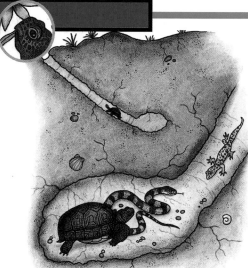

WHAT IT LOOKS LIKE

Gopher tortoises grow to be about 1 foot long.

The shell is a smooth dome. It is brown or black with rings. The underside is yellowish.

It has a horny spur on the front under the neck. The skin is orange to gray-brown.

The head is large and rounded.

The chubby legs are scaly. The toes are not webbed. They have claws. The tail is short and fat.

WHERE TO FIND IT

Gopher tortoises live in open, dry, sandy woods along the Gulf Coast from South Carolina to Louisiana. They also like scrubby beach areas.

They are out during late-morning, rainy or not. The rest of its time is spent in the burrow.

They are active all year and do not hibernate.

WHAT IT EATS

The gopher tortoise eats grasses, berries, fruits, seeds and leaves.

Tell an adult where you are going and how long you will be gone.

DESERT TORTOISE

WHERE TO FIND IT

Desert tortoises live in the canyons and dry rocky hillsides of Nevada, California, Utah and Arizona.

They are active at midday and late afternoon and after a summer rainstorm.

They spend much time in their burrows. In cold weather, desert tortoises hibernate in group burrows.

WHAT IT LOOKS LIKE

Desert tortoises grow to be about 12 inches long.

The domed shell is black to tan. It may have brown or orange marks. The underside is black to tan with some yellowish blotches and dark lines.

The neck skin is yellowish, the large, round head is tan to red.

There is a horny spur sticking out from the front of its underside.

The brown legs are chubby. The toes have claws. The tail is short and thick.

INTERESTING FACTS

Desert tortoises are endangered in some states.

Desert tortoises can live a whole year without drinking any water.

WHAT IT EATS

Desert tortoises eat desert flowers, cacti, grasses and berries.

Take this book and a pencil along when you go exploring.

GREEN TURTLE

WHERE TO FIND IT

Green turtles live in the Atlantic Ocean from Maine to the Florida Keys. They are also found from Alaska southward in the Pacific Ocean. They feed near shallow river mouths like San Diego Bay and around island groups, such as Hawaii.

They are active in these shallows in morning and late afternoon. Green turtles do not hibernate.

WHAT IT LOOKS LIKE

Green turtles can grow to be 4 feet long and weigh almost 900 pounds!

The olive-brown to black shell often has brown blotches. The underside is white or yellowish.

The skin is brown to gray-black. Its head is small.

The legs look like flippers. There is one claw on each foot. The tail is short and thick.

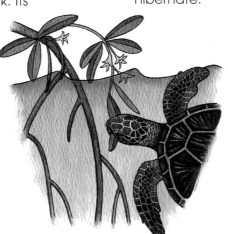

WHAT IT EATS

Green turtles eat turtle grass and other sea plants, algae and red mangrove roots and leaves.

Don't disturb turtle nests or hatchlings.

MAKE A TURTLE PAPERWEIGHT

You can keep a "turtle" in your house by making this fun paperweight. Try using different sizes of paper plates for little turtles and big turtles.

WHAT YOU NEED

- A sheet of newspaper

- Two matching paper plates with smooth, flat edges (not rippled)

- A cup of clean, dry pebbles

- A bottle of white glue

- Crayons

- Scraps of green or brown felt

- Scissors

WHAT TO DO

1 Spread the newspaper over your work area.

2 Using the crayons, color the bottom of one paper plate in your favorite turtle's shell colors.

3 Color the bottom of the other paper plate to be your turtle's underside.

4 Lay the paper plate for the top shell colored-side down.

5 Pour the pebbles into the middle of it.

6 Spread a thick layer of glue along the edge of the paper plate.

7 Lay the other paper plate, colored-side up, over it so the flat edges touch. Press the two edges to seal. Let dry.

8 Use the scissors to cut the felt scraps into shapes for the head, neck, tail and feet.

9 Glue them in place on the bottom of your turtle. Let dry.

Turn your turtle over.

It is now ready to sit in a special place.

SCRAPBOOK

Frogs, Toads and Turtles

Find All Kinds of Stuff . . .

Take-Along Guides

Titles available in the Take-Along Guide series:

Berries, Nuts and Seeds
ISBN 978-1-55971-573-7

Birds, Nests and Eggs
ISBN 978-1-55971-624-6

Caterpillars, Bugs
and Butterflies
ISBN 978-1-55971-674-1

Flamingos, Loons
and Pelicans
ISBN 978-1-55971-943-8

Frogs, Toads and Turtles
ISBN 978-1-55971-593-5

Planets, Moons and Stars
ISBN 978-1-55971-842-4

Rabbits, Squirrels
and Chipmunks
ISBN 978-1-55971-579-9

Rocks, Fossils
and Arrowheads
ISBN 978-1-55971-786-1

Seashells, Crabs
and Sea Stars
ISBN 978-1-55971-675-8

Snakes, Salamanders
and Lizards
ISBN 978-1-55971-627-7

Tracks, Scats and Sign
ISBN 978-1-55971-599-7

Trees, Leaves and Bark
ISBN 978-1-55971-628-4

Wildflowers, Blooms
and Blossoms
ISBN 978-1-55971-642-0

NorthWord
Minnetonka, Minnesota